POETRY

April 2012

FOUNDED IN 1912 BY HARRIET MONROE
VOLUME CC · NUMBER I

CONTENTS

April 2012

POEMS

FROM 100 YEARS

POETS WE'VE KNOWN

COMMENT

COVER ART BY MILTON GLASER
"Pegasus," 2011

POETRYMAGAZINE.ORG

A PUBLICATION OF THE
POETRY FOUNDATION
PRINTED BY CADMUS PROFESSIONAL COMMUNICATIONS, US

Poetry · *April 2012* · *Volume 200* · *Number 1*

Poetry *(*ISSN: 0032-2032*) is published monthly, except bimonthly July/August, by the Poetry Foundation. Address editorial correspondence to 61 W. Superior St., Chicago, IL 60654. Individual subscription rates: $35.00 per year domestic; $47.00 per year foreign. Library/institutional subscription rates: $38.00 per year domestic; $50.00 per year foreign. Single copies $3.75, plus $1.75 postage, for current issue; $4.25, plus $1.75 postage, for back issues. Address new subscriptions, renewals, and related correspondence to* Poetry, *PO 421141, Palm Coast, FL 32142-1141 or call 800.327.6976. Periodicals postage paid at Chicago, IL, and additional mailing offices.* POSTMASTER: *Send address changes to* Poetry, *PO Box 421141, Palm Coast, FL 32142-1141.* *Double issues cover two months but bear only one number. Volumes that include double issues comprise numbers 1 through 5. Indexed in "Access," "Humanities International Complete," "Book Review Index," "The Index of American Periodical Verse," "Poem Finder," and "Popular Periodical Index." Manuscripts cannot be returned and will be destroyed unless accompanied by a stamped, self-addressed envelope, or by international reply coupons and a self-addressed envelope from writers living abroad.* *Available in braille from the National Library Service for the Blind and Physically Handicapped. Available on microfilm and microfiche through National Archive Publishing Company, Ann Arbor, MI. Digital archive available at JSTOR.org. Distributed to bookstores by Ingram Periodicals, Source Interlink, Ubiquity Distributors, and Central Books in the UK.*

POEMS

PATRICIA KIRKPATRICK

Vision Test

The brain, like the earth, lies in layers.
Floaters dart and punch. I see the field.
My face stays numb. *Keep your eye on the target.*
Click the button when a light appears.
Last night I read "*So little evidence is left*
of what had vanished." I can't always follow directions.
The tumor pressed a lobe, charging
the amygdala, emotional core of the self.
In school they taught us that soil covers core
and mantle; mythology explains creation
and change. Now age drapes childhood;
my hair, the incision. I see a light but forget
to click. I didn't remember dreams for a year.
How I've changed may not be apparent.

Survivor's Guilt

How I've changed may not be apparent.
I limp. Read and write, make tea at the stove
as I practiced in rehab. Sometimes, like fire,
a task overwhelms me. I cry for days, shriek
when the phone rings. Like a page pulled from flame,
I'm singed but intact: I don't burn down the house.

Later, cleared to drive, I did outpatient rehab. Others
lost legs or clutched withered minds in their hands.
A man who can't speak recognized me
and held up his finger. I knew he meant
One year since your surgery. Sixteen since his.
Guadalupe wishes daily *to be the one before*. Nobody
is that. Sometimes, like love, the neurons just cross fire.
You don't get everything back.

In Extremis

You don't get everything back.
Is today morning or night? The radio voice says
the composer is changing the place home is.
When they try to put a tube down her throat,
the woman beside me sobs. Nurses probe
a vein as she thrashes, call the Hmong translator.

Once a boy told me, in Laos he sat in a tree
all night. *Father pay me dollar for every man I'm shooting.*
When there's water to cross, the fish, caught,
get needled through gill slits. Down the dark hall,
machines bleat at each bed. Eyes open and shut: flashes,
detachment, vitreous gel. Her son, seven years old,
comes after school, peels oranges, watches football,
changing the place home is.

NATE KLUG

Work

It hides its edges
in speed, it has
no edges. Plus every time
he thinks he knows

it close enough, can discriminate
centripetal force
from what gets sheared
straight off,

direction changes:
through stunned space the blade
snaps back,
turtles into its handle

and starts over spinning
the other way.
All along the chopped-up sidewalk
(the need to keep

breaking what we make
to keep making)
the concrete saw
plunges and resurfaces,

precise as a skull;
it glints against
the small smoke
of its own work.

Wisconsin

By new names
and then no names
at all, their laws
will reach your land,

Lorine, to feed
on your much loved
marshy spaces
whose occasional faces

discern a stranger
from far off
but like to take
a break from well

or welding just
to talk. We can-
not extricate
a place from those

it's made of, the sounds
it makes. But now
from Blackhawk
Island to Madison

to Washington,
geologies
thin; more things
sound or work

the same. Their laws
will reach your land,
Lorine, by new names
then no names at all.

HAILEY LEITHAUSER

Bad Sheep

Midnight's merely blue,
but me, me, me, I'm
through
and through
sloe, cracked soot-
on-a-boot,
nicotine spat, licorice whip.
You can scratch, scratch, scratch
but I stay underskin true
to ebony, ink, crowberry, pitch;
hoist me up by my hooves
and shake till I'm shook, I'm still
chock full of coke, fuliginous
murk.
O there's swart in my soul,
coal by the bag,
cinders and slag,
scoriac grit, so please
come, comb
through my fleece with hands pallid
as snow and watch
how they grow tarry, raven,
stygian, ashed —
or, if you wish, clean me with bleach
I won't
flinch, just char
down to a core of caliginous
marrow,
pure carbon, atramentous,
utterly piceous,
shadowed, and starless,
each clumpity clump
and eclipse of my heart raptly
re-burnishing
a woolgather dark.

RICK BAROT

The Wooden Overcoat

It turns out there's a difference between a *detail*
and an *image*. If the dandelion on the sidewalk is
mere detail, the dandelion inked on a friend's bicep
is an image because it moves when her body does,

even when a shirt covers the little thorny black sun
on a thin stalk. The same way that the bar code
on the back of another friend's neck is just a detail,
until you hear that the row of numbers underneath

are the numbers his grandfather got on his arm
in a camp in Poland. Then it's an image, something
activated in the reader's senses beyond mere fact.
I know the difference doesn't matter, except in poetry,

where a coffin is just another coffin until someone
at a funeral calls it a *wooden overcoat*, an image
so heavy and warm at the same time that you forget
it's about death. At my uncle's funeral, the coffin

was so beautiful it was like the chandelier lighting
the room where treaties are signed. It made me think
of how loved he was. It made me think of Shoshone
funerals, where everything the dead person owned

was put into a bonfire, even the horse. In that last
sentence, is the horse a detail or an image? I don't
really know. In my mind, a horse is never anywhere
near a fire, and a detail is as luminous as an image.

The trumpet vine on the sagging fence. The clothes
in the fire. And each tattoo that I touch on your back:
the three-part illustration of how to use chopsticks,
the four-leaf clover, the clock face stopped at 12:05.

EDUARDO C. CORRAL

In Colorado My Father Scoured and Stacked Dishes

in a Tex-Mex restaurant. His co-workers,
unable to utter his name, renamed him Jalapeño.

If I ask for a goldfish, he spits a glob of phlegm
into a jar of water. The silver letters

on his black belt spell *Sangrón*. Once, borracho,
at dinner, he said: Jesus wasn't a snowman.

Arriba Durango. Arriba Orizaba. Packed
into a car trunk, he was smuggled into the States.

Frijolero. Greaser. In Tucson he branded
cattle. He slept in a stable. The horse blankets

oddly fragrant: wood smoke, lilac. He's an illegal.
I'm an Illegal-American. Once, in a grove

of saguaro, at dusk, I slept next to him. I woke
with his thumb in my mouth. ¿No qué no

tronabas, pistolita? He learned English
by listening to the radio. The first four words

he memorized: In God We Trust. The fifth:
Percolate. Again and again I borrow his clothes.

He calls me Scarecrow. In Oregon he picked apples.
Braeburn. Jonagold. Cameo. Nightly,

to entertain his cuates, around a campfire,
he strummed a guitarra, sang corridos. Arriba

Durango. Arriba Orizaba. Packed into
a car trunk, he was smuggled into the States.

Greaser. Beaner. Once, borracho, at breakfast,
he said: The heart can only be broken

once, like a window. ¡No mames! His favorite
belt buckle: an águila perched on a nopal.

If he laughs out loud, his hands tremble.
Bugs Bunny wants to deport him. César Chávez

wants to deport him. When I walk through
the desert, I wear his shirt. The gaze of the moon

stitches the buttons of his shirt to my skin.
The snake hisses. The snake is torn.

JASON GURIEL

A Magnetic Personality

marc-antonizes.
Somehow it organizes
the mob — like so
much lead — into rank
and file. Somehow
it stands us
rabble up and makes
a row of men stiffen
or a rose of lead filings
arise. A rose is a rose
that arose, a magnetic
personality very
nearly said. She knew
how to draw
this one painter
to her place in Paris
and make him something
greater. (She knew
how to cube him.)
But the magnetic
can turn on
a dime and go
all red like a face
of a Rubik's Cube.
In fact, its flip
side can repel what it
once sucked in —
all those friends,
Romans, countrymen,
cubists.

John Hancock's John Hancock

makes wind
the way it whirls
about and blows
the neighboring names
of other signatories
away. The point
of it is not
the John or Jane
Doe it names;
the point's the quill
in motion as if
still stuck
and aquiver in
goose skin.
The trick to writing
well isn't up
the sleeve. It is
the sleeve
that fluffs up
the flourish,
that blooms around
the stunted stamens
of the fingers
and distracts us
from our grasping
for the sun
or the uncertain
scratching
of the stylus.

YUSEF KOMUNYAKAA

Snow Tiger

Ghost sun half
hidden, where did you go?

There's always a mother
of some other creature
born to fight for her young.

But crawl out of your hide,
walk upright like a man,
& you may ask if hunger is the only passion
as you again lose yourself
in a white field's point of view.

In this glacial quiet
nothing moves except —
then a flash of eyes & nerves.

If cornered in your head by cries from a cave
in another season, you can't forget
in this landscape a pretty horse
translates into a man holding a gun.

Omens

Her eyelids were painted blue.
When she closed her eyes the sea
rolled in like ten thousand fiery chariots,

leaving behind silence above & below
a thousand years old. He stood beneath
a high arched window, gazing out

at fishing boats beyond the dikes, their nets
unfurled, their offshore gestures
a dance of living in bluish entourage.

He was only the court's chief jester.
What he said & did made them laugh,
but lately what he sometimes thought he knew

could cost him his polished tongue & royal wig.
He was the masked fool unmasking the emperor.
Forget the revelation. Forget the briny sea.

He had seen the ravishing empress naked
in a forbidden pose. Her blue eye shadow.
Aquamarine shells crusted with wormy mud.

Anyway, if he said half of what was foretold,
the great one would become a weeping boy
slumped beneath the Pillars of Hercules.

Islands

For Derek Walcott

An island is one great eye
gazing out, a beckoning lighthouse,
searchlight, a wishbone compass,
or counterweight to the stars.
When it comes to outlook & point
of view, a figure stands on a rocky ledge
peering out toward an archipelago
of glass on the mainland, a seagull's
wings touching the tip of a high wave,
out to where the brain may stumble.

But when a mind climbs down
from its high craggy lookout
we know it is truly a stubborn thing,
& has to leaf through pages of dust
& light, through pre-memory & folklore,
remembering fires roared down there
till they pushed up through the seafloor
& plumes of ash covered the dead
shaken awake worlds away, & silence
filled up with centuries of waiting.

Sea urchin, turtle, & crab
came with earthly know-how,
& one bird arrived with a sprig in its beak,
before everything clouded with cries,
a millennium of small deaths now topsoil
& seasons of blossoms in a single seed.
Light edged along salt-crusted stones,
across a cataract of blue water,
& lost sailors' parrots spoke of sirens,
the last words of men buried at sea.

Someone could stand here
    contemplating the future, leafing
through torn pages of St. Augustine
    or the prophecies by fishermen,
translating spore & folly down to taproot.
    The dreamy-eyed boy still in the man,
the girl in the woman, a sunny forecast
    behind today, but tomorrow's beyond
words. To behold a body of water
    is to know pig iron & mother wit.

Whoever this figure is,
    he will soon return to dancing
through the aroma of dagger's log,
    ginger lily, & bougainvillea,
between chants & strings struck
    till gourds rally the healing air,
& till the church-steeple birds
    fly sweet darkness home.
Whoever this friend or lover is,
    he intones redemptive harmonies.

To lie down in remembrance
    is to know each of us is a prodigal
son or daughter, looking out beyond land
    & sky, the chemical & metaphysical
beyond falling & turning waterwheels
    in the colossal brain of damnable gods,
a Eureka held up to the sun's blinding eye,
    born to gaze into fire. After conquering
frontiers, the mind comes back to rest,
    stretching out over the white sand.

PATRICIA LOCKWOOD

The Arch

Of all living monuments has the fewest
facts attached to it, they slide right off
its surface, no Lincoln lap for them to sit
on and no horse to be astride. Here is what
I know for sure:

Was a gift from one city to another. A city
cannot travel to another city, a city cannot visit
any city but itself, and in its sadness it gives
away a great door in the air. Well
a city cannot *except for Paris*, who puts
on a hat styled with pigeon wings and walks
through the streets of another city and will not
even see the sights, too full she is of the sights
already. And within her walk her women,
and the women of Paris looking like
they just walked through an Arch …

Or am I mixing it up I think I am
with another famous female statue? Born
in its shadow and shook-foil hot the facts
slid off me also. I and the Arch we burned
to the touch. "Don't touch that Arch a boy
we know got third-degree burns from touching that Arch," says my mother sitting
for her statue. She is metal on a hilltop and
so sad she isn't a Cross. She was long ago
given to us by Ireland. What an underhand
gift for an elsewhere to give, a door
that reminds you you can leave it. She raises
her arm to brush my hair. Oh no female
armpit lovelier than the armpit of the Arch.

V. PENELOPE PELIZZON

Nulla Dies Sine Linea

On my birthday

A crow guffaws, dirty man throwing the punch of his
one joke. And now, nearer, a murder

answers, chortling from the pale hill's brow.
From under my lashes' wings they stretch

clawed feet. There the unflappable years
perch and stare. When I squint, when I

grin, my new old face nearly hops
off my old new face. Considering what's flown,

what might yet fly, I lean my chin
on the palm where my half-cashed fortune lies.

DAVID LEHMAN

The Breeder's Cup

I. TO THE FATES

They cannot keep the peace
or their hands off each other,
breed not yet preach
the old discredited creed.

Love is charity conceived
as a coin dropped
in a beggar's cup.
Reason not the need.

Gluttony is no nicer than greed
or wrath, but lust
is our categorical must.
We have no choice but to breed.

II. OLYMPIA

Olympia lies on her couch
with an insolent stare,
her hand hiding her crotch,
a flower in her hair.

She splits the lot of us with a sneer:
we are either breeders or queer.
We will fight wars because of her.
She will root us on. We will win.

The face in the mirror is not brave,
but we crave contact with her skin
and the jewel in the mouth of her cave.
She tempts like a sin

and under her spell we fall
into a deep enchanted sleep,
and wake up ready to make the leap,
ready to heed her call,

only now we're alone,
on streets less friendly than wilderness,
a platoon of ex-pals in Manhattan.
Olympia tempts like a sin,

but then sends us home to the wife,
commands us to resume the life
we had planned to give up in her honor:
the life of a dutiful husband, a modest success

in his profession, impressive
in credentials, in mood depressive
(but nothing that a pill won't cure).
You ask if he is happy? "Sure."

And Olympia lies on her couch,
with her insolent stare,
her hand hiding her crotch,
a flower in her hair.

SEAN HILL

Bemidji Blues

For Arnold Rampersad

Shadows bluing the snow, the pines' and mine,
bear the cast of a kestrel's blue-gray crown
I note as I find my way about this town.

Blues here more likely the Nordic-eyes kind
than the blue-black of some Black folk back home.
Here so many lakes reflect the sky's blue dome;

some summer days skimmed-milk blue tints windblown
whitecaps. Blue's an adjective, verb, and noun,
and the color of the world when I pine

because she's gone leaving too much wine and time.
Blue shadows on the snow, mine and the pines'.
For a tall man, blue ox, and now me, home

is Bemidji, though the blues here around
more the cast of a kestrel's blue-gray crown
than the blue-black of my cousins back home.

MICHAEL COLLIER

Six Lines for Louise Bogan

All that has tamed me I have learned to love
        and lost that wildness that was once beloved.

All that was loved I've learned to tame
        and lost the beloved that once was wild.

All that is wild is tamed by love —
        and the beloved (wildness) that once was loved.

SANDRA SIMONDS

You Can't Build a Child

with the medicinal poppies of June
nor with Celan's bloom-fest of dredged stone,
not with history's choo-choo train of corpses,
not with Nottingham's Robin Hood
nor Antwerp's Diamondland.

Not walking on the Strand in Manhattan Beach with her
silicone breast implants, refinery, waves of trash,
not out of the Library of Alexandria
with her burnt gardens that prefigure gnarly,
barnacle-laden surfboards broken in half.

You can't build the child with the stone paths
that we have walked on through the atmosphere,
the pirate's plank, the diving board, the plunge,
nor with the moon whether
she be zombie or vampire.
Not with Delphi, not with fangs, or cardamom bought
in Fez, red with spring, red with
marathon running cheeks.

Not with monk chant, bomb chant,
war paint, not with the gigantic Zen pleasure zones,
nor with this harnessed pig
on the carousel that I am sitting on with my son
in Nice, France. How it burns on its axis
as if it were turning into pineapple-colored kerosene
the way the Hawaiian pig, apple in snout, roasts
in its own tropical meat under the countdown sun.

ANTHONY MADRID

Once upon a Time

Once upon a time,
There was a beautiful shark.
She combed her long, blonde hair,
And it made the halibut bark.

It made the chicken oink,
And the whale to run for Congress.
A man should never obstruct
The course of material progress.

Yet a lamb cannot but weep
When the kiddies come home from college.
For they have forgotten to keep
The agreement they made to acknowledge

The woodpecker's right to peck,
And the maple's to be pecked at.
Let's have a little respect
For Rubber Duck with a doctorate.

That provocative way of standing!
All elbows and bangles
And hips just like a coat hanger
And ankles at right angles! I like

The shape of the pouring soy milk,
The sound of the splitting log.
But Egret finds it regrettable that her
Sister is dating a dog.

Don't listen to 'em, kid!
And don't listen to their questions.
This corporation's been ruined by
Well-meaning false confessions.

And the world is fast a-melting,
Though I would have it slow.
And I don't think it's helping:
The way these animals go

Straight from hatchery to quackery,
And, if only to amuse,
I'll throw my hat in with Mike Thataway in
Black patent leather shoes.

Maybe I'm just like my mother.
She's never satisfied.
Maybe I'm just like my father:
Always a bridesmaid, never a bride.

Maybe I'm just like my cat:
Licking invisible balls.
Perhaps you'll reflect upon that,
Next time you're screening your calls.

And all the solvent and the solute,
They were walking hand in hand.
This the Indian poets were the
First to understand.

The ancient Indian poets
Had their heads screwed on straight.
Fixed on the body's affluence
And the effluents that escape.

And the influence they enjoyed?
Close-focus hocus-pocus.
And every *gezunte moyd*
In a juvenile honey locust

Will prefer their Hindi distichs
To the Indiana Hoosiers.
We're gonna be there from Spit Christmas
All the way to Mucus New Year's.

But for now I draw the curtain
And settle into Lent.
Last person to go to Harvard
Without knowing what that meant.

AMIT MAJMUDAR

Horse Apocalypse

Hrhm Shp, colt-culling,
Is what hoof lore calls it —
The choke-chain sound a roan coined
To describe the things he saw
Before the sniff weevils crept
Up his nostrils and chewed
His eyes at the hue-sweet root.

•

Mother mares scare foals
From folly-trots and foxglove
By telling them fury tales
Of muck stirrup-deep and shells
Shoveling Passchendaele
Onto Passchendaele,
The foal fallen with the boy.

•

One memory, common
To all breeds, spurs night mares
Sparking down the mute streets
Of their sleep, gas-blind
Witnesses scraping Krupp
Guns over the cobblestones,
Winged sparks breeding in the hay.

•

Having watched us box and ditch
Our dead, they thought our dead
Ate termite-runnels
In the black bark of the land
And pulled all horsefolk down
To join whatever dark cavalry
Thundered underground.

•

The burlap gas mask cupped
And strapped to the wet snout
Could be mistaken, when
The gas gong sounded
And the men grew fly-heads,
For a feed sack chock-
Full of red ants.

KAREN AN-HWEI LEE

Song-Riddle: Asian Box Turtle

Questions for a zoologist
starting with anatomy
concluding with love:

Is a turtle's skin loaned?
True or false: weight of his shell
is lighter
than the light of drums.

What is the under-shell
and is it tough as a mangrove?

Can he see through his shell-box?
Can he see out the rear
to this sea of ours?

Does he exist in the order of things?
How does life begin, when does it end
and is that good or evil?

Yellow margin over a cuttlebone,
domed carapace
is it a lonely world

of sow bugs, cutworms, and God?

Song of the Oyamel

On the other side of this door

You are an oyamel native to the mountains of Mexico

Rising in a cloud forest of sister evergreens
Shedding pollen cones, shedding winged seeds

Our lost wings
singly and in pairs.

This is why the monarchs vanish
Raising sienna-hued colonies longer than my arms

Hibernating in Mexico where it's hotter in January
than my front yard, where the red bougainvillea raves

And magnolias with a mauve rush on paper
And open as though thinking about last year's novels

Read over the shoulders of garden-strollers

Obey the apostle's exhortation
And do everything in love.

KATHY NILSSON

Little Ice Age

I have one good memory — a total

Eclipse of the sun — when out of brilliance

Dusk came swiftly and on the whole

At seven years it felt good on a summer afternoon

To be outrun by a horse from another century —

The next morning I washed up

On land like a pod of seals

Struck with a longing for dark at noon —

If the cessation of feeling is temporary

It resembles sleep — if permanent, it resembles

A little ice age — and the end of some

Crewelwork by a mother who put honey

Into my hands so the bees would love me.

Still Life

I'm having trouble looking animals in the eye.

Their empty suits in outer space!

Monkeys injected with a virus to show off

Our eminent domain, the nervous system.

Teacup pigs we breed and obsessive mice

Worrying themselves bald in a miniature opera.

For pleasures of the tongue we are

Winking cattle out of meadows

Slashing their throats and swiftly quartering them.

In riding habits with gold flame pins we ride horses

To hounds, chase a fennec fox until his red

Coat flares up against the extinction

Of light. Once in a circus we made

An elephant disappear and he did not mind.

WENDY VIDELOCK

!

Dear Writers, I'm compiling the first in what I hope is a series of publications I'm calling ARTISTS AMONG ARTISTS. *The theme for* ISSUE 1 *is "Faggot Dinosaur." I hope to hear from you! Thank you and best wishes.*

—*Ali, editor,* Artists among Artists

I think that I shall never fear
a brontosaurus that is queer,

iguanodon as fetisheer,
a mammoth bringing up the rear,
an astrodon with extra gear,

metrosexual squirrel and deer,
a breeder with a dance career,
a fruit with cauliflower ear,

a lesbianic Chanticleer,
a grinning limpish-wristed Lear,
the weird one or the mutineer,

but those who perfectly adhere,
stay clear, stay clear, stay clear, stay clear.

BEVERLEY BIE BRAHIC

Reunion: J-School, Class of 19--

Cutlery clatters into the sink.
But always the characters, uniquely themselves,
only some decades older. They search
for their coats. You were, she reminds him,
our resident nomad, come to pitch your tent
here, sidewalks for sand, unaccustomed taboos:
Morningside Heights, one of your lives.
Thirty years
since the awkward goodbye? Before he goes —
East Africa his beat, Germany hers — he'll
visit the nephew, the namesake in Boston
who drives a cab, sends a pittance each month
to a wellhead in — we'll call it *Sudan*.
He explains how it works, this drip feed
of cash to *Sudan* from the *United States*:
cheap, fast. She's not clear about this — he jots
her a website: it's a place she can go.
So they won't meet again ... suddenly
Can you forgive me? he blurts —
a classmate's apartment, Upper West Side,
the grown child's room, bears
in tidy shrines, scrum of sloughed coats.
In the kitchen friends wash up. Sound
of laughter. Sound of water flowing
out of a tap. *Yes*, she replies, shocked
by the twinge, then ache, of remorse.
She "*forgot*"? And him — thirty years —
the place still hurts? *It's myself I can't forgive*,
she knows later. Right now, vague shame.
End of *March*. Maybe *April*. Street trees
are trying to bloom. The irretrievable
sits on the table, white as a plate. He holds her
her coat.

TARA BRAY

Numbered

The girl was known for shitting in her yard.
I did so little for her. She was small, a dandelion orb
with ragged hair like an old woman's burnt from dye.
Her face showed little sign of poverty —
it was her dusty shoes cut open at the top that told.
A bone look she'd mastered young, yet the curve
of her face was edible, like a rounded sparrow in hand.
She wasn't mean, but did what she wanted — quietly,
with a lift to her chin, while I struggled to teach her anything.
I'd like to say I brushed her brittle hair, called her beautiful,
coaxed out sight words that dawdled on her tongue.
I dream of her spinning like a fairy dervish in my failure.
Consider this a prayer, a foolish one.

ELLERY AKERS

Hook

One year a general
packs the dead arithmetic in a drawer—
all the subtractions, divisions.
The next year, vines cover the bunkers.
The brain resumes its starbursts of rehearsal.
The heart leaps under the defibrillator.
The bone eases into its socket.
Skin grows back. Scars fade. Eyes clear.
Look at the trees at the burn, six years later.
Look at the sprout on a hay bale
on a truck. Look at the woman who was raped,
had her hands cut off in a creek:
She's getting married.
The choir sings. The bride smiles.
The groom slips a ring on her hook.

FROM 100 YEARS

In the course of reading poems to include in an upcoming centennial anthology of work from our pages, we found ourselves appreciating more poems than could be included in the book. Throughout the coming year, we will feature selections from past issues that illuminate current content, but won't appear in *The Open Door: One Hundred Poems, One Hundred Years of* Poetry *Magazine*. What follows are poems and letters that dovetail with "Poets We've Known."

GEOFFREY HILL

Wreaths

I

Each day the tide withdraws; chills us; pastes
The sand with dead gulls, oranges, dead men...
Uttering love, that outlasts or outwastes
Time's attrition, exiles appear again,
But faintly altered in eyes and skin....

II

Into what understanding all have grown!
(Setting aside a few things, the still faces,
Climbing the phosphorus tide, that none will own)
What paradises and watering-places!
What hurts appeased by the sea's handsomeness!

May 1957

MURIEL RUKEYSER

Song

Make and be eaten, the poet says,
Lie in the arms of nightlong fire,
To celebrate the waking, wake.
Burn in the daylong light; and praise
Even the mother unappeased,
Even the fathers of desire.

Blind go the days, but joy will see
Agreements of music; they will wind
The shaking of your dance; no more
Will the ambiguous arm-waves spell
Confusion of the blessing given.

Only and finally declare
Among the purest shapes of grace
The waking of the face of fire,
The body of waking and the skill
To make your body such a shape
That all the eyes of hope shall stare.

That all the cries of fear shall know,
Staring in their bird-pierced song;
Lines of such penetration make
That shall bind our loves at last.
Then from the mountains of the lost,
All the fantasies shall wake,
Strong and real and speaking turn
Wherever flickers your unreal.

And my strong ghosts shall fade and pass
My love start fiery as grass
Wherever burn my fantasies,
Wherever burn my fantasies.

April 1955

Song for Dead Children

We set great wreaths of brightness on the graves of the passionate
who required tribute of hot July flowers —
for you, O brittle-hearted, we bring offering
remembering how your wrists were thin and your delicate bones
not yet braced for conquering.

The sharp cries of ghost-boys are keen above the meadows,
and little girls continue graceful and wondering.
Flickering evening on the lakes recalls those young
heirs whose developing years have sunk to earth,
their strength not tested, their praise unsung.

Weave grasses for their childhood — who will never see
love or disaster or take sides against decay
balancing the choices of maturity.
Silent and coffined in silence while we pass
loud in defiance of death, the helpless lie.

October 1935

GWENDOLYN BROOKS

Gay Chaps at the Bar

… and guys I knew in the States, young officers, return from the front crying and trembling. Gay chaps at the bar in Los Angeles, Chicago, New York …

Lt. William Couch in the South Pacific

We knew how to order. Just the dash
Necessary. The length of gayety in good taste.
Whether the raillery should be slightly iced
And given green, or served up hot and lush.
And we knew beautifully how to give to women
The summer spread, the tropics, of our love.
When to persist, or hold a hunger off.
Knew white speech. How to make a look an omen.
But nothing ever taught us to be islands.
And smart athletic language for this hour
Was not in the curriculum. No stout
Lesson showed how to chat with death. We brought
No brass fortissimo, among our talents,
To holler down the lions in this air.

November 1944

"Still Do I Keep My Look, My Identity . . . "

Each body has its art, its precious prescribed
Pose, that even in passion's droll contortions, waltzes,
Or push of pain — or when a grief has stabbed
Or hatred hacked — is its and nothing else's.
Each body has its pose. No other stock
That is irrevocable, perpetual,
And its to keep. In castle or in shack.
With rags or robes. Through good, nothing, or ill.
And even in death a body, like no other
On any hill or plain or crawling cot
Or gentle for the lilyless hasty pall
(Having twisted, gagged, and then sweet-ceased to bother),
Shows the old personal art, the look. Shows what
It showed at baseball. What it showed in school.

November 1944

HOWARD NEMEROV

Political Reflection

loquitur the sparrow in the Zoo

No bars are set too close, no mesh too fine
To keep me from the eagle and the lion,
Whom keepers feed that I may freely dine.
This goes to show that if you have the wit
To be small, common, cute, and live on shit,
Though the cage fret kings, you may make free with it.

September 1956

To the Mannequins

Adorable images,
Plaster of Paris
Lilies of the field,
You are not alive, therefore
Pathos will be out of place.

But I have learned
A strange fact about your fate,
And it is this:

After you go out of fashion
Beneath your many fashions,
Or when your elbows and knees
Have been bruised powdery white,
So that you are no good to anybody —

They will take away your gowns,
Your sables and bathing suits,
Leaving exposed before all men
Your inaccessible bellies
And pointless nubilities.

Movers will come by night
And load you all into trucks
And take you away to the Camps,
Where soldiers, or the State Police,
Will use you as targets
    For small-arms practice,

Leading me to inquire,
Since pathos is out of place,
What it is that they are practicing.

November 1961

CORRESPONDENCE

The influential British poet, critic, and editor Geoffrey Grigson (1905–1985) published a "Letter from England" in the November 1936 issue of Poetry *in which he disparaged the work of Dylan Thomas, C. Day Lewis, David Gascoyne, F.R. Leavis, and others; though he praised a number of writers including W.H. Auden, Stephen Spender, and Christopher Isherwood, Grigson wrote that he mostly found "a jelly of mythomania, or self-deception, careerism, dishonesty, and ineptitude." The "scarcest quality among young English writers," he wrote, was "integrity." The piece triggered a vigorous correspondence between Grigson and the estimable William Empson.*

Dear Sir:

Somebody ought to explain about Grigson, when he introduces himself to a new circle of readers, as he apparently did in the November *Poetry*. The trick of being rude to everybody is, of course, paying journalism of a certain kind, but in Grigson it also comes from the one honest admiration discernible in him, for the work and methods of Wyndham Lewis. However, Grigson shows no sign of having any theoretical basis to be rude from, which Lewis has plenty of; nor has Grigson any capacity in poetry himself; published partly under an assumed name, Martin Boldero, his stuff has been pathetic. This of course need not stop him from being rude to good effect, and he has a good journalistic nose for what he can safely be rude to. But it is annoying to have him call people "climbers" when no other brickbat seems handy. Grigson himself is the only climber in the field. Not that a climber is anything very shocking; but he has got himself a comfortable job as critic by nose and noise alone. He may have published some decent criticism which I have not read, but in his magazine he does not so much as pretend to give reasons for insulting people. (He has not attacked me; I had rather a sharp review in his paper from someone else, but that was criticism all right.) Of course apart from this "climber" talk it is a good thing to have someone making a lively noise, but someone else, as he points out, ought to say Boo.

The coxcomb bird, so talkative and grave,
Who from his cage calls cuckold, whore, and knave,
Though many a passenger he rightly call,
You hold him no philosopher at all.

W. EMPSON
JANUARY 1937

To the Editor of *Poetry*:

You observe: say one word about writers in England, stick in one millimeter of pin, and out come petulance and squeal, for that is all that Mr. Empson's letter is made of. "The trick of being rude to everybody.... paying journalism of a certain kind.... a good journalistic nose for what he can safely be rude to.... a comfortable job as critic by nose and noise alone"—very neat, very delicate, but wouldn't Mister Empson have used your space a little more sensibly, in *replying* to my "Letter from England"? Is there or is there not, a remarkable inertia masquerading in England as activity? Do English writers, or do they not, form defensive fronts of the fifth-rate? Do David Gascoyne and Dylan Thomas and F.R. Leavis and Michael Roberts, and Herbert Read, and Day Lewis, et al., deserve, or do they not deserve, the things I said about them? Mr. Empson, ranging himself with the Sitwells as an *English gentleman*, might have stood up for his friends, if he had had anything to write beyond innuendoes and exaggerations about *New Verse*. For must the reason for insult always be stated? Can it never be obvious? And does not "nose" contradict "everybody"? Mr. Empson is right; I am not rude (if he must have the word) from "any theoretical basis." I attempt to be rude—a typically inert theorizer and poetical *pasticheur* of Mr. Empson's kind would scarcely see it—I say, I attempt to be rude from a moral basis, a basis of differentiating between the fraudulent and inert and the active, genuine, and desirable. The inert verbalism in which Mr. Empson deals may not be fraudulent, but it has always, if Mr. Empson would care to know, struck me as quarter-man stuff so unreadably trivial that it is not worth insulting or attacking.

GEOFFREY GRIGSON
MAY 1937

To the Editor of *Poetry*:

The important thing here seems to be the anti-intellectual stuff. I wouldn't want to deny that it lets Grigson put up a case; in fact, that is the danger of it, that it will defend anything. For instance, it is a bad thing to be a quarter-man, but it is a great sign of being a quarter-man if you strut about squaring your shoulders and seeing how rude you can be. And it is necessary to make your final judgments "on a moral basis," but if you haven't done some thinking *first*, your moral intuitions will as like as not be mistaken and harmful. If you set out to forget simple truths like these it gets easy to be proud of yourself for being manly and moral.

The anti-intellectual line can be a useful defense for valuable things; a man like D.H. Lawrence had a right to it. But as to whether the fifth-rate (not that I agree about who is fifth-rate) form defensive fronts — they do, they do; and this is one of their fronts.

WILLIAM EMPSON
MAY 1937

POETS WE'VE KNOWN

WILLIAM LOGAN

Geoffrey Hill

I arrived in England shortly after the Brixton riots and in the midst of the Ashes, won largely through the heroics of Ian Botham. He was a legend then—a decade later, when he could neither bowl like a demon nor hit for six with the old careless, magisterial command, it was said that the legend had become a myth. Over the streets, nailed to hoardings, were large signs that advised TAKE COURAGE. Courage was a brand of ale. It was high summer, 1981.

Debora Greger and I had rented a modest terrace house in Cambridge on a back street near the river, an apple tree in the garden and a chiropractor next door. Up and down the Cam trailed the stately swans, dying of lead poisoning. Because we knew no one, I dropped notes to local poets and critics—I suppose that's what Eliot did when he arrived in London almost seventy years before. The only poet in Cambridge, so far as I was concerned, was Geoffrey Hill. A note was returned, asking me to come on a certain afternoon to his rooms in Emmanuel College.

Hill was not quite fifty, slightly barrel-chested, with a dark scurf of beard. He lodged in a small set of rooms up one of the staircases in a modern wing of the college—the rooms were neither austere nor overdressed. Hill was courtly in his coolness, but he took boyish pleasure in showing off the knickknacks and arcana displayed on a coffee table. He was proudest of the small pistol his father had carried as a police constable in Bromsgrove. I mentioned that I had been reading a lot of Larkin. "Larkin!" he exclaimed from the little kitchen, where he had gone to fix us a drink. "That yobbo!"

For the two years we lived in Cambridge, we met Geoffrey for lunch every month or so, or invited him to dinner on Pretoria Road. He dressed in black, like some English Johnny Cash, except for a pair of lurid socks—fuchsia and acid yellow were favorite colors, the rakish touch in that monkish wardrobe. Each time it was as if we were meeting as strangers. He would be stiff, heavy with a formality that lasted a quarter hour or so; then at last, by infinitesimal degrees, he would warm to the company (or just give in to the burden of friendliness). Once he did a wicked imitation of a hedgehog.

Hill was breathtakingly shy, nearly as shy as a hedgehog — formality and bluster were his protections against the world. We attended three or four of his lectures, which were grave, learned, delivered as if composed of death notices — they were also ponderously slow. (By the end of a series of lectures, only a few true believers were left in the hall.) His method, which did not endear him to students, revealed the pressure of learning within, while tending to hide the grace. Indeed, that seemed part of the poet's character — he was not an example of grace under pressure, but of pressure under grace.

There were also, I now recall, one or two Dinky toys on that table, additional relics of his childhood. (These perhaps make more important the references in poems to his toys.) "I am certain," he once admitted, "that on a back street, in a cathedral town, there stands a shop, its windows coated in dust. Inside there are still shelves of old Dinky toys, pristine in their original boxes, and bearing their original prices."

Toward the end of 1982, Hill loaned us the typescript of *The Mystery of the Charity of Charles Péguy*. He mentioned that, where he had changed his mind, he had tried to find a word of the same number of letters, so the compositor wouldn't be put to trouble. When I foolishly pointed out that different letters took up different amounts of space, he looked crestfallen, as if some terrible secret had been revealed.

Faced with the petty annoyances of life, Hill often adopted a rueful tone. Once, in the upper stacks of the university library, he came round a corner, having loudly pronounced his irritation at not being able to find some book crucial to a footnote. Seeing me with my head buried in a book, he stopped short. "You are always there," he said, "to observe my inadequacies and misdemeanors." I no longer recall what prior accident had elevated me to that status — but then the dryness was his way of being funny.

We both had a taste for rare books, acquired on the cheap. One day something went wrong with his car, and I offered to look at it. My competence as a mechanic may be dubious, but there was some complication in the fuses I was able to figure out — and soon the thing was running again. In celebration, he decided to drive us into the fens to a bookshop in the horse-racing village of Newmarket, a shop long heard of but never visited. Geoffrey's fantasy was that we would discover there a pristine copy of *Land of Unlikeness*, probably for tuppence.

This was perhaps not as impossible as might appear. On the 50p table at a local bookseller's, I had found the original edition of *Typee*, and on the shelves of another shop a signed copy of Bret Harte stories for £6. Indeed, there was a tale circulating in Cambridge of a man who, visiting a dusty bookshop in Prague or Budapest, no doubt on a back street, had spirited away a copy of the Second Folio for a couple hundred pounds. Our appetites had been whetted. We arrived at the shop. The door was locked. A hand-lettered sign on the glass read "Closed Due to Death of the Owner." As we turned away, Geoffrey muttered, "The man knew we were coming... and died." Then he smiled.

We left England late in the summer of 1983. As a farewell, Geoffrey invited us to lunch at Emmanuel, a departure from custom, as he preferred to meet in pubs. Having greeted us in his rooms, he led us down to the dining hall. Before we entered, he turned and said, with courtly gravity, "If I do not introduce you, it is only because I... have forgotten... your names."

Those were about the last words spoken between us for a quarter-century. In time, somehow or other, I ended up with two copies of *Land of Unlikeness*.

GERALD STERN

Muriel Rukeyser

I was reading Muriel Rukeyser, along with Roethke, Lowell, Berryman, and Thomas for years, and I went to her readings when I was in New York, but I never met her until we gave a reading together at the Walnut Street Theatre in Philadelphia, in 1976. She was, at the time, sixty-three years old — and "famous"; I was fifty and just starting to gather a reputation. She was there with her friend, Monica McCall, and greeted me with a huge smile and careful observation of my clothes and my companions, my wife Pat and my eighteen-year-old daughter Rachael. She made a comment about the elbow patches on my wool jacket — in this case, as I pointed out to her, sewed on by Pat to cover the holes — and proceeded to call me "Mr. Poet." I accepted the nomenclature, as I explained the patches and kissed her on the forehead. As if to test me, she insisted she would read first, which I dismissed outright by a shake of the head and a gesture of the arm.

The room we read in was on the top floor of the building. It was long and narrow — very long, I remember — and held an overflow audience of, I would guess, over two hundred people. She kept dropping the sheets of paper in which her poems were typed and rather than pick them up she just went on, impromptu. They asked us questions afterwards and one well-dressed fool kept pestering me about my "Jewish vision," as he called it. I said — after a while — sotto voce, "I don't want to be mean," to which Muriel, standing beside me, said, "be mean, be mean" — which I did. Which I was.

I met Muriel the next spring — 1977 — at the Roethke Poetry Festival at Lafayette College in Easton, Pennsylvania, an hour and a half from New York. Roethke had taught at Lafayette — his first teaching job, in the thirties. He was also the college tennis coach. He used to drive down the Delaware River to visit Stanley Kunitz on his farm near New Hope, Pennsylvania where they read their poems to each other. The festival was named for him, certainly in ironic memory of his short tenure there. I was teaching a poetry workshop at the time at Lafayette and each year I was responsible for choosing the poets for the festival. The others that spring were David Ignatow, Etheridge Knight, and C.K. Williams. I remember the gorgeous reading Muriel gave, her talk, and the hour we spent alone. She and Ignatow got on a bus together in front of the Easton Hotel for the trip back to New York.

Jonathan Galassi, my editor then, had asked Muriel to write a blurb for *Lucky Life*, published in the fall of 1977, and I made a trip to New York (from Easton) to release her from that burden, given the state of her health; but sitting at her kitchen table over a cup of tea she told me, word for word, what she was going to say. I wrote a poem called "Rukeyser" detailing that visit, especially her nurse's anger when she came back from shopping and saw Muriel out of bed, only a thin shawl covering her shoulders, and talking — heatedly — as she did.

The last time I saw her was at the group reading of Kit Smart's "Jubilate Agno" at the Church of the Transfiguration on lower Fifth Avenue, which Galway Kinnell organized and years later wrote about in his gorgeous poem "Jubilate." We each read a section from Smart's poem. Allen Ginsberg, James Wright, Philip Levine, Jane Cooper, Etheridge Knight, Grace Paley, myself, and ten others. Muriel, the last reader, fell slowly down at the microphone, a mini-stroke, dizziness, confusion. She had been sick for almost fifteen years, and would die soon after. Galway related, in his moving — and comic — lines, how she sank slowly to the floor, still reading, and insisted only on a chair, refusing both doctor and ambulance, reciting the last lines of her portion from a prone position, the wires and the microphone in a heap on top of her.

It was 1978, two years after the publication of her last book, *The Gates*, containing her narrative of the visit to Seoul to stand vigil — as president of PEN America — at the gates of the prison where the Korean poet Kim Chi-Ha was confined, without papers or pen, for speaking up against the South Korean government. For writing. *The Gates* also contains her poem, "St. Roach," the unbelievable reaching out to "the other," in this case the disgusting and the filthy, as we commonly perceive it, a poem whose greatness, in terms of content as well as music, is still to be fully realized. She was groundbreaking, earth-shaking, stubborn, and visionary. It was a great honor to have known her.

PATRICIA SMITH

Gwendolyn Brooks

At first glance, she couldn't even strain toward remarkable. In Chicago, there were legions of colored ladies who looked, moved, sounded just like her. Peppering the street-corner markets, they listened intently to the melons, gathered collard leaves into ragged bundles, shooshed flies away from browning bananas. In the hot middle of some Tuesday, they rode the clacking "L" train, squinting at posted maps during the entire trip, terrified at the thought of missing Pulaski or Garfield. They wore stockings two shades too drooped, the sturdy kind that latched to girdles, although the thick hose always seemed to be wound down to a fat roll just beneath their knees. Their eyes were shutting down, gradually dimming everything the sun did, and they pushed Coke-bottle specs up on their noses with wrinkled forefingers while they glared knowingly at you, fast gal, full as you are with the world.

They were the aunties, the m'dears, the ladies who pressed heads, those sweet whatever-their-names down the street from the Baptist church. They were the warm, insistent presence, a lack of electric. Once you focused and realized they were there — standing in front of and behind you in some line, chortling loud and off-key during Sunday service — there was a comfort about them. Just how they kept being everywhere.

On that blustery February day Gwendolyn Brooks, looking like so many colored ladies of a certain age, of a certain dusted stature, seemed a very small part of the chaos surrounding her. Blues Etc., one of Chi's most storied music haunts, smelled like whiskey and winking, and on that day it was filled with people who were filled with words. For five full hours, beginning in the afternoon and seeping into midnight, dozens of poets would cross the rickety stage on their way to the mic. The event, "Neutral Turf," was a benefit for Guild Books, a venerable Chicago institution. It was also a balls-out attempt to pull together members of Chicago's fractured poetry community, which was in the midst of an unprecedented growth spurt. In its burgeoning midst were slammers and academes, formalists and freestylers, adolescents and orators, finger-pointers, ruthless competitors and unrepentant cravers of limelight. Everyone insisted that whatever *they* did was hotter, doper (that was a word then), more literate, relevant, contemporary, the next big thing. The organizers of Neutral Turf had devised an embarrassingly simple plan: get everyone mildly plastered and just giddy enough to realize that they were all doing the same damn thing.

I'm ashamed to admit it now, but I had come without words. My goal, as I remember it, was to drink heavily and laugh at poets. It was winter, which meant that Chi was a windy little ivory hell, and a five-hour respite—complete with blinking neon, warm drinks, and hilariously overwrought metaphors—was definitely in order. OK, I was young. I assumed poetry was relegated to a dusty bookshelf that I couldn't and didn't care to reach. I planned to guffaw heartily at odes to soulful flowers clawing their way up through cracks in the concrete.

I didn't know it yet, but Ms. Gwen was havin' none of that. She sat in the front row, head scarf triangled and tied, stockings rolled, specs riding her nose. I'm not sure how I knew she was who she was. (Later I learned that every Chicago colored girl is hardwired to recognize Gwendolyn Brooks on sight.) She paid rapt attention to just about every poet, smiling and nodding to rhythms, and making a small "O" sound when a line or phrase reached her in *that way*. During breaks, she nurtured the newbies, hugged when a hug was warranted, sipped at something icy and bland. Three of the five hours had passed, and she was still there, present in the soft but insistent way of the colored woman. Everywhere, gently, brashly.

When I approached her, I wasn't sure what I wanted. On a break between poets, I moved close and began, "Miss Brooks, I—" But a dreadlocked young woman—whose musical name, Inka Alasade, I remember to this day—had stepped to the mic and was about to begin her poem. Miss Brooks smiled and turned away from me to face the stage and listen. But she never let go of the hand I had extended in greeting: *I'm here. I'll be back. I am a vessel for what you need to say.*

So I held tight to what I did not yet know was a lifeline. I had come to drink and laugh out loud at a language I didn't think I needed to know, and now I held on as that language flowed from her fingers to mine.

I held on far beyond the eventual continuation of our conversation, during which I would begin to know poetry as necessary breath. I held tight past that day, that neon-splashed room, the procession of both fledgling and comfortably-rooted writers. I clutched that knowing hand while my city finally acknowledged poetry as its heartbeat, as fractured elements forged an alliance and began to build one of the country's most formidable and adventurous creative communities. And in the center of that community, I burned like an ember, almost consumed by discovery.

I was from the West Side, the part of Chicago everyone tells you to stay away from. Gwendolyn lived on the South Side, where I was raised to believe the "bourgeoise" blacks resided. In Chicago terms, that can be two sides of a cultural and economic abyss. But I saw her often, usually at readings and events sponsored by Guild Books. In my hunger to be suddenly and completely immersed in all things literary and Chicago, I had volunteered to shelve books there on weekends. I met Eduardo Galeano. Guffawed heartily with Studs Terkel. And finally got to have my first real, unhurried conversation with Gwendolyn Brooks.

"I remember you," she said, just over my shoulder.

I turned around and hugged her, just like that. It was a rash, spontaneous clutch, a way to greet a childhood friend or a lost-ago aunt, not exactly the recommended hello for a casual acquaintance who just happened to be a former poet laureate and official Queen of the Colored Girl. For the moment, those three words legitimized me. She could conceivably have remembered me for my tendency to respond out loud at readings to poems that moved me, or for my habit of sitting up front and center, gazing gape-mouthed at my heroes. Maybe she was recalling Neutral Turf. But I wanted to think that she'd been in an audience somewhere and that I'd been on stage, that she'd heard something I said, and that she liked it. I wanted to believe that, so I didn't ask, just in case the answer was elsewhere.

We stood in a shadowed corner of the place while the busyness of a revolutionary bookstore went on around us. She pulled volumes down to show me, to tout the writer, to point to a favorite passage. We talked about Don L. Lee, Sterling Plumpp, Angela Jackson, Margaret Burroughs. I displayed an appalling lack of knowledge about what and who had come before me.

In my head swirled unrooted verses waiting for me to believe in them. My very first book, *Life According to Motown*, was still years away. It would be very much a first-generation-up-north book, a Chicago girl book, the first effort of a "stage poet" on the page, and it would come to exist primarily for two reasons:

1) Chicago stalwart Luis Rodriguez started Tia Chucha Books and asked me if I had a manuscript. Even though I didn't, I said yes.

2) What Gwendolyn Brooks said to me that day in Guild Books.

I had uttered something that countless other writers have uttered before, a silence-filler of sorts, a throat-clearing that I assumed Ms. Brooks, and anyone else who had ever picked up a pen, would instantly relate to and agree with. I was craving the comfort of common ground when I said, "I have a real problem finding time to write."

The corner of her mouth twitched, then spread into one of those indulgent smiles that knots you up a little inside. It's the smile a teacher gives you before handing back a test paper with a grade lower than either of you expected.

Without looking directly at me, Gwendolyn said, "Your problem should be finding time for anything else."

Silence, then. We continued to pluck certain books from certain shelves, examine glossy covers, read a little to ourselves. More people poured in, the program began, and she was quietly brilliant. When it was over and she was gone, I went home to my poems.

My poems, which suddenly *were* my home.

MAXINE KUMIN

Howard Nemerov

In the mid-sixties, while I was teaching freshman composition part-time at Tufts University, Howard Nemerov unexpectedly came into my life. Because the university's senior poet, X.J. Kennedy, was away on leave, it fell to me to introduce the visiting bard to his audience. This was to happen at 4 PM on a cold December afternoon. I was told to meet him in the parking lot thirty minutes before his reading and accompany him to the auditorium.

It never occurred to me that someone who was a full professor and had already published three books — all of which I owned — could be anxious about giving a reading. I was nervous about how to introduce myself, but he was so visibly agitated that I simply said who I was and asked him what he would like to do.

Tufts sits atop a drumlin. The lot where we met lies at the bottom. What Howard wanted to do was walk away his pre-reading jitters. It was windy and cold. Snow was predicted by nightfall. We walked up the hill, then down. Then up and down again. I think we did this three times until on the stroke of four we entered the auditorium. I said a few words and a masterful Howard Nemerov took the podium.

We shared that story a few times over the years, meeting serendipitously at writers' conferences and symposia. I remember one event at the Library of Congress where the matter under discussion was how to make poetry more accessible to the public. Howard leaned across the table and offered sotto voce, "I say let's not. Let's keep it a secret."

But of course he didn't favor opacity. His style was meditative, witty, often ironic, sometimes acerbic but always intelligible. He was offended by the sprawl and brawl of Allen Ginsberg's poems. I shudder to think what comments he might have offered if he had lived long enough to encounter the Language poets.

Here he is, in a wry six-liner from *The Western Approaches* (1975) titled "Strange Metamorphosis of Poets":

> From epigram to epic is the course
> For riders of the American wingéd horse.
> They change both size and sex over the years,
> The voice grows deeper and the beard appears;

Running for greatness they sweat away their salt,
They start out Emily and end up Walt.

Another passage, from "Make Love Not War" in *The Blue Swallows* (1967), is even more pertinent today. Written in a relaxed, more-or-less pentameter line, it showcases Howard's wry, mordant wit:

Treasury officials have expressed grave concern about
The unauthorized entry of stateless babies without
Passports and knowing no English: these "wetbacks,"
As they are called from the circumstance of their swimming
Into this country, are to be reported to the proper
Authority wherever they occur and put through channels
For deportation to Abysmo the equatorial paradise
Believed to be their country of origin.

In 1978 I served as a visiting professor at Washington University in St. Louis, where Howard had been a faculty member since 1961. (In 1999, eight years after his death, a new residential building on the campus was named after him.) Howard took me to see the avenue of gingko trees on campus, famous for dropping their leaves all in one night. He took me to the zoo. I came often to supper, before which Howard savored his extra dry martinis (and highballs after). Peggy, his English WWII bride, was horrified to learn that I had never eaten Yorkshire pudding. She promptly mounted a large dinner party featuring the traditional menu: roast beef, the famous pudding, and Brussels sprouts. Dessert was trifle, which I did not dare confess I had also never tasted.

Howard died of esophageal cancer in 1991. No dying friend had ever phoned me before to say goodbye. He had just had his vocal cords sprayed with a Teflon-like substance, he told me, so that he could keep a final speaking engagement. I was too stunned to do more than utter platitudes.

After he was gone I found that he had made many farewell calls, including one to Julia Randall. "Hard to get a tan here," he told her, "in the valley of the shadow."

Could anyone muster a riposte to that?

CLIVE JAMES

William Empson

In England in the sixties and seventies I was often out and about leading the literary life, and I met a surprising number of my heroes without really seeking to. The real surprise, each time, was that they were all in character. One night in Hull I was performing a cabaret act in the student bar and it turned out that the dour adult figure sitting at the back was Philip Larkin. Later on he told me that he was so deaf he hadn't heard a word, and I was too dense to ask him why, in that case, he had come. In London I saw a lot of Kingsley Amis and he was almost never not irascible. He could talk enchantingly for hours about abuses to the language but if he caught you abusing it he would always give you what for on the spot. Robert Lowell was in London for a while and I had several opportunities for observing just what a handful he could be. I thought he was a nitwit, but strictly in the sense that he was normally something else, and turned dippy only when the wind changed.

William Empson was well-known to have been wildly eccentric from the beginning. It would have been a tough reputation to live up to at a first meeting, but when I finally did bump into him in Cambridge one night he effortlessly soared off the scale of weirdness into a realm I had not previously encountered. He was giving a reading in the Cambridge Union and I — still a graduate student, so it was a great honor — was one of the support readers. A few lines into his first poem he started explaining it, and his explanation became so abstruse that he shifted from side to side. He was on the point of walking in circles when I offered to help. As I remember things now, I would read a stanza of the poem and then he would start explaining again. It all took forever and gave the audience plenty of opportunity to study his beard, which was at that time in a phase when it all occurred below the level of the chin, as if he had stuck his head through a rug. We support readers were cut down to about five minutes each but he was very kind about a poem of mine, and started explaining it to me.

Since I thought the world of his work, I took this as a high compliment. But he wasn't yet through with his largesse. From a side pocket of his jacket he produced a crumpled plastic sack which had obviously been in there for some time. The contents were well crushed, but with typical precision he identified them. "Would you like a crisp?" I took a few fragments and chewed. They tasted very old, like flakes from the wall of an ancient Egyptian tomb. I was beginning to get the idea that the verbal titans might not necessarily be models of sanity. Later on this perception came in handy for the vital and continuing task of not setting unreal standards of normality for yourself when you are engaged in an activity quite so strange as pushing words together into patterns and expecting people to listen to them.

I have never met the greatest of my heroes, Richard Wilbur. Everything I have ever read about him contributes to the picture of a man who can start his career staring German Panzer divisions in the face and yet still achieve work that is a miracle for its clean, sane poise. Once, in London, not long after I arrived there, he gave a reading at the American embassy and he was so preppy, so perfectly Phi Beta Kappa, that he glowed like an icon. As I write this he is getting old but in his latest photographs he still looks like a film star: one of the sane film stars, like James Stewart. Yet knowing what I know about all my other heroes, I won't be surprised to hear that when they clean out his attic they will find it full of plastic bath toys.

There again, Empson's principal advantage had been that there was nothing to discover. Quite early in his adult life he had established it as standard practice that he would make sexual advances to people of either gender as long as they never washed, for example. Nothing came as a surprise except, on the night I met him, one thing: the batty, hair-framed face was fully concentrated on you as if you yourself were one of the scientific phenomena in one of his marvelous poems. If you were still at the stage of doubting your own identity, it could be unsettling to meet someone who seemed not to doubt it at all. He was really tremendously interested in what I thought of the crisps, so I chewed my mouthful with a show of connoisseurship, thinking: Try to say something interesting, this guy is a genius.

COMMENT

SVEN BIRKERTS

Emerson's "The Poet"—A Circling

For we are not pans and barrows, nor even porters of the fire and torch-bearers, but children of the fire, made of it, and only the same divinity transmuted, and at two or three removes, when we know least about it.

Thus Emerson, in "The Poet," one hundred seventy years ago. An expression that makes vivid the great paradox, which is that one and the same sentence can greet us as if from another world, even as it speaks with the intimate breath of someone leaning in to tell us something we feel we already knew. Which—here, now—is the point. Not that there is a gulf of time between us and Emerson, but that there might be an inner level at which we are contemporaneous. That this level would have little to do with dates and fashions goes without saying.

I feel as reluctant to write about this as I am interested. For what is clear to me right off is that there is no going forward if the word "soul" cannot be used. I see no point in talking about poetry in any deeper way without that access. At the same time, I know that there is no faster way to get cashiered out as the worst sort of throwback than by saying "soul" with a straight face.

What does this mean? Why should there be such discomfort around a word—or, rather, a concept? It's as if to use the word is to say at the same time that you are denying the age you live in, deliberately voiding history, as if the conception of soul cannot be squared with things as they are.

I should define the word, make clear how I mean it. To speak of soul is not, for me, to speak about religion; it is not to announce oneself as a church-goer, a born-again Christian, or anything of the kind. Soul, for me, is prior to religion. Religion recognized the idea and posited it as something that it could help save, but not as something that faith brought into being. Soul comes before. I think of it as the active inner part of the self, the part that is not shaped by contingencies, that stands free; the part of the "I" that recognizes the absurd fact of its being; that is not in any sense immortal, but that recognizes the concept of immortality and understands the desire it expresses; that *is* that desire.

Soul, considered in this way, is a quality that can be recognized in expressions of language, even though it cannot be explained or accounted for. That it can be recognized confirms that language can express it. Does rarely, but *can*. And the expressions most kindred, most likely — though still very rare — are poems. This is because poems are written out of a double intent: to give voice to the most urgent and elusive inner states, and to use language with the greatest compression and intensity. The most lasting poetry — speaking historically — is the poetry that has given some expression to the poet's soul, that part of him- or herself that connects most deeply and exactly with the souls of others.

•

But the great majority of men seem to be minors, who have not yet come into possession of their own, or mutes, who cannot report the conversation they have had with nature.

What an astonishing idea it is that Emerson has of the poet. Not so out of place if we think back to Shelley and his attributions of power, but head-shakingly baffling if we look from the vantage of the present. But these phrases are to be looked at, and closely: the idea that the great majority of people are *minors, who have not yet come into posession of their own*. What could this mean, in Emerson's terms and ours? What is it to "come into possession"? I don't think he means mere — "mere" — maturity. Rather, it seems that he is still on the theme of the soul, and that the possession refers to that — to a person's coming to recognize himself as a soul — something greater than the contingent sum of his parts, his experiences. And how might that recognition be accomplished? The next phrase may hold a partial answer: the idea that there might be, as a basis for this coming into one's larger self, a *conversation they have had with nature*. What kind of conversation would one hold with nature? Emerson does not mean us to picture his person, his would-be poet, yodeling about in the woods, talking to trees and rocks. Surely not. He must be thinking of a conversation one would hold with oneself, with that nature that is within oneself, that fire of creation he adduces in his opening passage. Which sounds a good deal like the pop catchphrase about "getting in touch with your deeper self." So vague as to mean almost nothing. Deeper self... But the question is there to be asked: is there such a thing? Is there still traction in the idea of the self having not just depth, but depth that at some fathom-level connects us to a primary element — said fire — in a way that then informs our living, gives us substance beyond all accumulations of the incidental and distracting. Further, is this a power that artists — not just poets — can somehow access? Is Emerson proposing self-knowledge as an active force, an attainment that can then lead to other attainments?

What interests me is that there is none of this kind of conversation to be found — not anywhere can it be found and recognized. Sure, there is always the private sphere, and what can happen between individuals in honest and searching conversation. Or therapy — good, intensive therapy. But so far as the public realm goes — academia included — there is none to be found. Academia, indeed, is part of the reason why there isn't, for it has fostered and entrenched a culture of embarrassment. Academia has set itself *against* the preoccupations, concepts, and the essential spirit of what Emerson is doing here. Inklings of it were, only a decade or two ago, still to be found in the literary sector, in so-called belles lettres, but those have vanished completely.

At issue, really, though it will take some circling around, is the power and place of the individual. Not the demographic self, but the seeking, self-apprehending "I" — and, secondarily, the poet. The poet because she traditionally represents the importance of the search and manifests it through expression, through words. Not words as denotating or pointing to experience, but words as containing and embodying its energy.

But who thinks of language in this way, who believes that power? Except maybe a handful of poets.

•

> *For poetry was all written before time was, and whenever we are so finely organized that we can penetrate into that region where the air is music, we hear those primal warblings, and attempt to write them down, but we lose ever and anon a word, or a verse, and substitute something of our own, and thus miswrite the poem.*

What a notion. It would appear, living as we do in an era where social reality is understood to be a construction, and the rest a matter of neural processing — another kind of construction — that we have come a full 180 degrees from Emerson's assertion, which is not only that order inheres in creation, but that truths do as well, and that to discern and transcribe these with complete accuracy would be to bring forward a perfect beauty. Beauty — art — being not creation so much as the recovery of implanted harmonies. The poet, then, is the vessel, and language is the medium. And the implication is that language is adequate, while the transmission can be more and less successful. In-dwelling truth, and words fit for its recovery. So that words can be said to partake in some way of that essential stuff, related to the "primal warblings."

As the editor of a literary magazine, I spend a good deal of time reading poetry submissions, assessing from my particular angle the state of the art. One of the things that has struck me — in the way that can only happen if you find yourself looking quickly (mostly) at a very large sample — is a quality of arbitrariness. I don't mean arbitrariness in terms of subject matter, or approach, but at the level of language. Word choice, rhythm — those qualities that signify whether one is in the near-presence of poetry long before thematic elements are considered. Though it would be hard to specify exactly how this works, I would say — never mind all the decades of experimentation and innovation we have seen the genre go through — that determining whether the language is being used with poetic pressure, whether the words and phrases and lines are charged with the intent to mean, is easy. This can be felt on the pulse; it is prior to other judgments. And the more you have exposed yourself to poetry, the clearer this is. Just as you can hear when an instrument is out of tune, or several instruments are not tuned to the same pitch, so you can feel when the words are in a deliberate and sympathetic arrangement. This does not mean that they have to be making harmony — there are artful dissonances that reflect this, too — only that they are being used with some high awareness of their implicit verbal properties, and the understanding that all verbal juxtapositions release their chemical properties, and that a poem does this with high deliberation. Though it often takes a number of readings to decide whether a poem really "works," it takes only a few seconds to decide whether the expression qualifies as a poem.

Whether this quasi-chemical understanding of words on the page has any relation to Emerson's proclamation about original creation — it would be hard to advance the argument — it does allow us to see poetic language as operating far more subtly, and with greater variation, than the language we use to make sure the day's business gets done. And to consider expression as open to all kinds of nuance is not to be making any argument about its enchanted origins. The magic need not be the property of the words themselves, activated through inspired use — it can also reflect our capacity to project upon words, when their arrangement elicits projection.

•

For, the experience of each new age requires a new confession, and the world seems always waiting for its poet.

It will be necessary to keep the sentiment but broaden the reference. That the world *seems always waiting* seems incontestable, the feeling of waiting is everywhere — it is, I think, what makes us ever more deeply enslaved to our devices: we are glued to our screens of all sizes not for amusement or business, but because we think something is going to be announced. We can't bear to miss it. But that something is not poetry, unless we give poetry an apocalyptic possibility. We are on the run from the anxious vibration of our living, caused in part by the sense that things are more connected than ever and that it's the whole world that is somehow pressing in on us, "obsessing our private lives," as Auden wrote, though the nature of those private lives has changed a great deal since that writing. It could almost be argued that we no longer have private lives, and that that lack, and the porousness that it implies, is the cause of our unease, is what underlies that waiting. We are waiting for something that will feel like a solution when it arrives; we are waiting for the oppression of "what's next?" to be lifted. We are, in a deeper sense, waiting for our poet. But we are not waiting for the poem so much as the permission to certify ourselves, to inhabit the world on terms we understand, to be free of the feeling that everything is being decided elsewhere. The poet, then, is the emblem of self-sufficiency, and the poem, could we only find our way to it and understand it, is his proof. The poem of our age, the new confession, would find a way to shape the ambient energies and the anxiety of that interconnectedness into an expression that felt contained, that gathered the edgy intuitions that pass through us constantly and made them feel like understandings. Not closed off or insistent understandings, but clarifications, ways of abiding with the terrifying glut of signals.

Moving that agitated flurry into language is no small task. It might even be impossible, given that the nature of most of these signals is pre- or post-verbal. Emerson's assertion becomes a question, *the* question: can anyone, poet or artist or mere lay mortal, create a confession—an expression, a synthesis—that would alleviate the waiting world? Or have we moved once and for all beyond the pale of synthesis—with only partial versions possible? Another way of asking whether our circumstance is now beyond the reach of vision. Beyond language.

How does the poet, the serious poet, navigate what has become the inescapable porousness, the basic destruction of the boundary of the private? Is the full and authentic lyric poem possible, or is it condemned to being a nostalgic gesture—with part of its impact derived from that fact?

•

> *Observe how nature ... has ensured the poet's fidelity to his office of announcement and affirming, namely, by the beauty of things, which becomes a new, and higher beauty, when expressed.*

What a stunning and redemptive thought! But it needs to be looked at: that the beauty of things becomes a new—and *higher*—beauty when expressed. We know expression to be a kind of transformation, if only of vague inklings and inchoate half-thoughts into syntactical propositions. But that the world's beauty is made new, augmented, by artistic expression—this would somehow argue that the form-conferring impulse of consciousness is not just a part of what *is*, but an advancement. I think of Rilke—his question in the *Duino Elegies*: "earth, isn't this what you want: to arise within us, *invisible*?" And isn't that the substance of the first of the *Sonnets to Orpheus*: nature re-forming into language through the poet's consciousness? *Tall tree in the ear.*

Be that as it may. What strikes me here is how archaic these sentiments seem, how remote from contemporary thinking, even by so-called "creative" types. To make such a claim for any art, to consider any making by the imagination to be an actual power. It seems a measure of how far we have conceded to the merely material.

I take Emerson's poet as the focus, but really I am talking about all the arts. Not about their aesthetic development, but about their perceived power within the cultural system. It seems to me they have nearly none. Prestige, sales, their place in whatever is the collective conversation: the arts are in receivership. The concerns and insights of these idiosyncratic makers do not bear on the lives we are anxiously leading. Could it be, at least in part, because they have not found a way to take that anxiety and its myriad sources and make of it a subject matter: to exercise upon it precisely that transformation that Emerson claims the poet can exercise upon the beauty of nature?

Part of the problem — part of what tells me that there is a problem — is that I want to speak of poetry and art in terms that sound foolish. Not just because of their idealistic seriousness (but wasn't this the idiom we learned was proper to this discussion) — it *sounds* embarrassing — but because works that might justify that sort of language do not come readily to mind. And perhaps because of that I always feel saddened when I hear the high-minded propaganda of arts organizations that are looking for ways to bring their wares before the public.

If art is no longer transformational, can it recover some part of that power? Is it of any interest to us if it cannot, except of course as curriculum fodder? The question, I suppose, is not whether art can make beauty at all, but whether works of art — paintings, novels, musical compositions, poems — can still exert significant effect on people, can alter the ways they think and live? Can they make sufficient beauty, beauty big enough, poignant enough, unsettling enough? I would ask, too, how much this process — this bringing into being of newly imagined forms — requires the belief of the maker in a potential audience? Can significant, impact-making beauty be created without faith that it might be received? How different it is to create when there is a felt need, a desire. Have we lost the wanting? And if we have, how could that have happened? Do we not take ourselves seriously as souls? Is that what is at issue?

•

Our science is sensual, and therefore superficial.

Two sentences earlier Emerson has written: "The Universe is an externization of the soul." Do we need to go quite so far? But some essential split, or disjunction, comes into view. The sciences do treat of the outer, superficial, *material* manifestations of things — by definition. And they consider all phenomena with reference to their type, their abstracted essence. This was Walker Percy's insight about the difference between the writer and the scientist: the scientist never addressed the individual.

If the arts are not exerting any serious effect, are not being hungered for (which is what has allowed us to come to such a pass), this might be because we are less and less experiencing ourselves individually and through an awareness of our lives as possessing depth. Less and less psychologically; less and less existentially. We are making ourselves increasingly amenable to the logics of sciences and systems that control our lives. Everything is subject to the demographic calculation, the logic of the survey, this all-pervasive voting on preferences ironically giving the illusion that we are making choices, expressing ourselves, being proactive.

The dying out of the arts, or of the idea of the power of the arts, is linked to this waning of the psychological "I," never mind anything as fanciful as the soul. It is not the fashion to speak in these terms, as it is not the fashion to address anything having to do with inwardness, or even to use words pertaining to it. Except when notched with irony. Try it. Go anywhere among consenting adults — except those of a born-again or overtly New Age persuasion — and use the words *soul, spirit, inner*... You will see that they have become toxic for public consumption. Where the words have been lost, the concepts cannot be far behind. Take away the concepts, the consensual awareness that gives them life, and you cannot hope to have the thriving of serious art.

•

A beauty not explicable is dearer than a beauty which we can see to the end of.

Here I'm surprised, this doesn't seem in keeping with the rest of Emerson's thinking. Can there be a beauty that we can see to the end of — is that a beauty? To me the quality that certifies the beautiful is that it exceeds explanation. A work completely laid to rest by analysis, with no over-and-above aspect, which doesn't even expose the mystery of its making, or all making, cannot possibly lay claim to beauty. After all: "Beauty is the beginning of a terror we are just able to bear" (Rilke) and, no less dramatically, "Beauty is truth, truth beauty" (Keats). But I'm fussing too much now. The important idea is that beauty is essentially unknowable, which is to say it is not a thing that merely greets the rational mind; it somehow reaches the senses and the emotions and the intuitions, all those other ways of knowing that we have.

But what is now the status of beauty? We don't appear to fetishize it as we have at various times in the past. I am almost never told, about any new art, that I must see it, that it's "beautiful." Exciting, yes, that I hear, along with: unsettling, provocative, unusual, intriguing, even sometimes *powerful*. Of course there are beautiful novels and poems being written, beautiful paintings painted. But they are so often works that hark back in some way. Renditions of the cultural present are almost expressive of some dissonance; they communicate as part of their message the fact of a falling away from former orders and understandings — those things that underwrote the earlier beautiful. Do we jettison the term, or do we repurpose it — in the interests of that Keatsian "truth" — to include much that has been considered ugly?

That "over-and-above" quality, that which does not yield to analysis, is not *explicable*; that is the object of the search — though, of course, it cannot by definition be had. But it can be referenced, pointed toward. It has everything to do with the subject: the poet, the artist, the condition of art. Music can be subjected to stringent analysis, it can be precisely notated, and yet the notations give no purchase whatsoever on beauty. Because while a note can be named, a sound, and from sound a melody, cannot. And with poetry, beauty and mystery begin at the very point where denotation ends. The meanings of the words reach the mind; the word sounds reach the senses. The primary material conditions for the making of beauty have not changed. But the frame of attention, and the context of mattering — these have. A poem, however lyrically brilliant, lies inert so long as its music cannot press its claim. For this there must be attention, and attention is only active as attention *toward*. It is created by a desire or a need. If we need meanings, we will attend to those things that may yield them.

The crisis of art — if it is a crisis — arises from a loss of attention, a falling off of that which creates attention.

•

Readers of poetry see the factory-village and the railway, and fancy that the poetry of the landscape is broken up by these; for these works of art are not yet consecrated in their reading; but the poet sees them fall within the great Order not less than the bee-hive, or the spider's geometrical web. Nature adopts them very fast into her vital circles, and the gliding train of cars she loves like her own. Besides, in a centered mind, it signifies nothing how many mechanical inventions you exhibit. Though you add millions, and never so surprising, the fact of mechanics has not gained a grain's weight. The spiritual fact remains unalterable, by many or by few particulars.

And here, maybe, is a way of grasping the problem of the "ugly," for there has been such a proliferation of "inventions" and such a spread of updated versions of the "factory-village," that the poetry of landscape has not so much been interrupted as displaced almost entirely. Which is how the old question of beauty has been overpowered by subject matter. Our life consists of materials that have not been assimilated. Where is the centered mind that can absorb all that we have wrought and make poetry — or any art — from it? If Emerson is right then the proliferation is just quantitative and it does not change the deeper principle: the "fact of mechanics" remains the same. But the quantity would seem to have distracted us, made it far more difficult to recognize the "spiritual fact." Again, it is attention that is at issue. The complexity of the technologized world has distracted us completely, made it hard to believe that there is anything else besides.

And if there were a poet — an artist — who had the breadth to take it all in, to subject it to a full human pressure, could there be the beginnings of a new beauty — "new styles of architecture, a change of heart" (Auden) — and if there were, could we rouse up enough attention to understand it as such? Must beauty await attention, or is part of its task to awaken it?

•

Language is fossil poetry.

What a philosophy is encoded in those four words. Original seeing, and the first coinings of likeness, matching of sound to object or action, signifier to signified, is itself poetry. Which is to say, again, that poetry is attention, is complete openness to experience. Perception before the first coat of familiarity, the inevitable reductions of received wisdom. The study of Greek—I've not attempted it—is said to feel like an excavation, a laying bare, bringing one closer to what over centuries has calcified, retaining the shape signature but not the sap of the living thing.

•

Banks and tariffs, the newspaper and caucus, Methodism and Unitarianism, are flat and dull to dull people, but rest on the same foundations of wonder as the town of Troy, and the temple of Delphi, and are as swiftly passing away.

We could substitute, say, mutual funds and the Internet, Twitter and Facebook, and maybe the principle would be the same. But I have to ask now, having given Emerson his high-toned say, whether these phrases, these assertions, strike any recognition. He is one of our bedrock thinkers, and his thought is on subjects that, being of the spirit and the supposed verities, ought not change that much over time. And yet it seems to me, reading, that we have landed on a different planet, that not only do the beliefs about the art match nothing that I have heard any artists talking about, but the conception of the human that is invoked is almost impossible to square with anything available in our secular marketplace. People don't talk this way, or think this way, not about poetry—or anything. Emerson's transcendental projections of the human may have marked a moment, one of those F. Scott Fitzgerald moments that imagines the promise of the new land and ties that imagining to an exalted vision of the individual, his possibility; but if it had any hope at all, the moment was undone by commerce and the external busyness of nation-building. I spend so much time with "The Poet" for this very reason: because nothing could be different, because we could not be more opposite. And yet to the poet there still accrues some trace of this hyperbolic endowment; the label—"poet"—still carries a tinge, as does that of "artist." If there is any space still kept for the unpredictable, the inward-looking, the singular, then it is signed over to these people. Assigned, and yet it is a kind of phantom-limb attribution. For we don't credit the inward as a place for progress or gain, or anything much at all. That the material order would be on some continuum with an immaterial "spirit"—even suggesting this would court ridicule.

VERA PAVLOVA

Heaven Is Not Verbose: A Notebook

My writing: hard-boiled. My life: scrambled soft.

•

The cud of thinking: by the evening my jaw aches.

•

An elderly poet called me "the most beautiful woman in the world" because he could not recall my name.

•

There are moments when I feel the universe expand.

•

Mandelstam: "Poetry is the certainty of being right." Brodsky: "Poetry is the school of uncertainty." I am not certain about either assertion.

•

—Mom, how much is 95 times 60?
—Liza, I am busy working on a poem. If it weren't for that, I could possibly give you the answer.
—And how much would it be?

•

Poetry should be written the way adultery is committed: on the run, on the sly, during the time not accounted for. And then you come home, as if nothing ever happened.

•

Time is like a diatonic scale: it consists of major and minor seconds.

•

Pick a piece of wood floating in the river and follow it down the current with your glance, keeping the eyes constantly on it, without getting ahead of the current. This is the way poetry should be read: at the pace of a line.

•

Went to bed with an unfinished poem in my mouth and could not kiss.

•

Inspiration: when I have confidence in myself.

•

—I will never use makeup as long as I live, and then at the funeral parlor they will put it on me!
—Not if you expressly forbid it in your will.
—Why should I? Let them: for once in my life I will look pretty.

•

To write in spite of everything, even when generally speaking there is nothing to spite.

•

On Yuri Gagarin, the first man in space: his last name comes from the Russian *gagara*, a flightless bird.

•

To help a poem hatch, I went to get some groceries. Paid the cashier, got my change, came home with a finished poem and no groceries.

•

How do I feel about people who do not understand my poetry? I understand them.

•

—Mom, on the exam should I play "March of the Wooden Soldiers" with inspiration or with no mistakes?

•

More and more often, I come around to the conclusion that my dad is the sole true censor and critic of my poems: seriously drunk, in the kitchen of our country house, he squints after each poem I read to him and says, "Crap. Next."

•

My ninety-year-old grandmother is hard of hearing; it took her a while to understand the news, and then she said: "If they gave such an award to our Vera, how lousy poetry must be these days!"

•

Being well-known means knowing almost nothing as to who knows you and what they might know about you.

•

Suddenly you realize that only what you have put into poems can be considered lived through. That is how you become a poet. And at that point you begin, consciously or otherwise, living the kind of life that is fraught with poetry. That is how you cease being human. The former happens abruptly, the latter gradually, both irrevocably.

•

From the memoirs of Akhmatova's last physician: she died at the moment when her cardiogram was being recorded. Her death has been recorded in the form of a straight line. Ruled paper ready-made. Go ahead and write.

•

"The ovaries of a newborn girl contain up to 400,000 egg cells." All my poems are already in me.

•

Poetry begins when not only the reader but also the author starts wondering whether it is poetry.

•

Not to envy others is easy. It is difficult not to feel pleased when they envy you.

•

In her homework ("Describe your room in 'Eugene Onegin' stanzas") Liza wrote: *some dolls and books are on the bed ...*
— That is not really true, because the books were on the shelves. But I put them on the bed, to make sure that my verses were true to life.

•

My love for Pushkin has something marital about it.

•

Any one of my poems fits on a palm of the hand, and many on a palm of a child's hand.

•

There is still so much room for happiness in my breast! And everywhere I look, I see quotations from my yet unwritten books.

•

Postmodernism: vulgarity trying to pass for irony.

•

In a poem a word is not equal to its meaning as it is defined in a dictionary, because either the meaning in a poem is totally different, or it is the same but a thousand times more precise.

•

Drafts in my notebook are written in a barely legible scribble; fair copies are in impeccable calligraphy. My handwriting is much better than my muse's.

•

I write to equalize the pressure from without and from within, to prevent being squashed (by misery) or being blown apart (by happiness).

•

Tolstoy: "Man should live as if a beloved child were dying in a room next door." As for me, I live as if that child were dying in my womb.

•

—Do you understand that understanding is impossible?
—I do.

•

In a poem, poetry is a guest. At times the guest stays long, but never for good.

•

I've asked myself: Did I get ahead of the calendar? Counted the poems I wrote this year: 366 of them.

•

By giving my books as presents, I mark my territory.

•

The primacy of poetry: in its origins, European prose goes back to *The Lives of the Troubadours*.

•

"You are my first and my last/Bright listener of the dark raving." — Akhmatova to her lover Garshin in "The Poem Without a Hero." After they broke up, she changed the line to "You, not the first nor the last/Dark listener of the bright raving." (From Lydia Chukovskaya's *The Akhmatova Journals*.)

•

"Understanding is insanity for two." (V. Podoroga)

•

I put words into poems the way I pack a suitcase for a trip abroad, choosing only what is the most necessary, the most presentable, the lightest, and the most compact.

•

Lying in a hot bathtub, I look for a line to finish a poem, find it, and feel cold shivers down my spine.

•

Madness is inspiration idling in neutral.

•

I live my life moving forward on rails that I lay myself. Where do I get the rails? I dismantle the ones I have gone over.

•

My diaries are letters from my former self to my future self. My poems are replies to those letters.

•

Prose: a soccer game shown in its entirety.
Poetry: the same game shown only in scoring or near-scoring episodes.

•

Reader: So you want me to feel as if I were reading a letter addressed to someone else?
Poet: I want you to feel as if *I* had read a letter addressed to you by someone else and am shamelessly quoting from it.

•

Inspiration is an intercourse with language. I can always tell when language wants me. I never say no to language. For me, it is always good with language. And for language? I am afraid for language it is never as good as it is for me.

•

"Accusing an erotic poet of depravity is as unfair as accusing a tragic poet of cruelty." (Evgeny Baratynsky in the preface to his poem "The Concubine.")

•

Stravinsky: "I like writing music more than I like music."

•

A poetaster's poems: karaoke singing.

•

As I am learning to speak English, I catch myself saying in it not what I want to but what I can say. Then I realize that much the same happens when I speak my native Russian. Only in poems, at times, I manage to say what I want. On such occasions, I feel I am speaking not Russian but some other language that is truly my native.

•

Just as I expected, everything has come out not the way I had expected.

•

—Wow, what are all those things you've got hanging in your toilet?
—Those are my awards.
—And what do you do for a living?
—I'm a poet.
And then we both went after our respective business at hand: the plumber proceeded to fix the commode, and I continued to make fair copies of poems.

•

In a dream Pushkin tells me: "The three sources of my writing are gramophone, frog, and nightingale."

•

A cowbell is the opposite of an alarm system: when you hear it, everything is fine; when you don't, something is wrong. My poetry is a cowbell, not an alarm system.

•

On how I relate to my reader: There is an acoustical anomaly in a vaulted hall at Grand Central Station in Manhattan. My reader and I are standing at the opposite corners of the hall, facing the walls, and I am reading my poems in a whisper. The two of us are separated by the moving crowd and the racket of the train station, yet I know that the reader can hear every one of my words. If he or she is still there.

•

A fisherman told me: "Writing poetry must be like digging for earthworms: you grab the critter by the end and pull. Pull too hard, and it'll break; not hard enough, it'll get away."

•

Brodsky: "Prose is infantry, poetry is air force." I would add: a translator is a paratrooper, a Green Beret.

•

If poems are children, poetry readings are PTA meetings.

•

You must not write in verse about what you do not know or about what you know for sure, only about what you vaguely suspect, hoping that poems will either confirm or dispel your suspicions.

•

From a letter of a young poet: "I write when I feel bad. When I feel fine, I don't write." With me, it's the opposite: when I write, I feel fine. I feel bad when I do not write.

•

I write about what I love. I love writing even more than what I write about. And what do I do it for? To love myself, if only for a brief while.

•

"Is there any need for poetry? The question in itself is enough to realize how bad the situation with poetry is at present. When everything is fine, no one has the slightest doubt that there is absolutely no need for poetry." (B. Pasternak)

•

A poet who speaks of himself speaks of any man. Any man who speaks of a poet speaks of himself.

•

A slip of the tongue cannot happen to a poetaster. In poetry, to commit such a slip you need to have a tongue to speak with.

•

Rules in poetry can be broken, but that should be done with gusto, without looking back, the way D. drives his Ferrari on the highways of Europe: so much over the speed limit that radars cannot catch him in their photo frames.

•

What is the difference between destiny and hype? Destiny has better taste.

•

Cleanliness kills identity: K.'s wife washed her hands so frequently that eventually they would leave no fingerprints.

•

I know all my poems. It's just that some of them I have already recalled, and some not yet.

•

Truly beautiful are those who are not afraid to seem ugly. The same holds true for poems.

•

Towards the end of his life Mikhail Kuzmin, one of the best Russian poets, believed he was truly knowledgeable only in three fields: Gnosticism, music of the period between Bach and Mozart, and the Florentine Quattrocento.

•

A new collection by a great poet: when I was reading it with my eyes, the words chirped and hopped on the page; when I was reading it aloud to S., the words died in flight one by one. S.: "There is a category of classified documents called 'Eyes Only.' Highly secret!"

•

According to the rules of Tuvan throat singing, only the soloist can sing in polyphony, whereas the choir must sing in unison. Polyphony in the choir is perceived as singing out of tune.

•

The sense of life is in living to the fullest the moments when life seems to make sense.

•

A Swiss winemaker told me that rose bushes are planted along the edges of vineyards not for embellishment but to alert about blight: being sensitive, roses become blighted long before the grapevine does. That is when I understood that Andersen's "The Princess and the Pea" is not about being spoiled, but about the difference between a true poet and an imposter.

•

An ideal poem: every line of it can serve as a title for a book.

•

"In his books, and only in his books, a writer can do anything he pleases, provided he has talent. In real life, however, a writer cannot be overly lax, so as not to let people guess that in his books he tells the truth about himself." (L. Shestov)

•

Reader: Do you want me to recognize my everyday world in your poems?
Poet: No, I want your world to seem unfamiliar to you, once you take your eyes off the text.

•

—I have the gift of finding lost things, such as a tiny screw from sunglasses in thick grass of a lawn. I have a method of my own: I relax and wait until the lost object calls out to me: "Here I am!" Things like reading glasses, a notebook, an elastic hair band ... I can recognize them by their voices!
—But isn't that the way you write poems?
—How true! Except that with poems I never know what's been lost. All I know is that a) it's something urgently needed; b) something that is somewhere near, probably in the most visible of places; c) others have failed to find it; and d) it'll be such a joy when I do!

•

Only in poetry can it happen that words affirm, rhythm negates, syntax doubts, while the poet does not know who is in the right. And even if he does, he won't say.

•

Reading poetry in public is a form of betrayal. Having been entrusted with terrible secrets, I blurt them out, share them with total strangers, and thus let down the keepers of secrets who may lose confidence in me.

•

In the beginning, S.'s superiors used to tell him: "You need to smile more when you're working!" My mentors used to tell me: "There is not enough pain in your poems." At the time S. was working as an interpreter at oncology hospitals. I was writing about happy love.

•

When a true poet dies, we realize that all his poems were about death.

•

The longer a poem, the weaker the impression that it has been dictated from above: Heaven is not verbose. Besides, the more you talk, the more you lie.

•

Reader: Yevtushenko claims that in Russia a poet is something more than just a poet. Is that true?
Poet: No, nothing can be more than a poet.

•

A full stop at the end of a poem is an exclamation mark seen from above, driven into the page up to its cap with one precise blow.

Translated from the Russian by Steven Seymour

CONTRIBUTORS

ELLERY AKERS* is a poet, novelist, essayist, and visual artist. She is currently at work on a book of nature essays and a collection of poems. She lives in Northern California.

RICK BAROT has published two books of poems with Sarabande Books: *Want* (2008) and *The Darker Fall* (2002). He teaches at Pacific Lutheran University and Warren Wilson College.

SVEN BIRKERTS is the author, most recently, of *The Other Walk* (Graywolf Press, 2011). He is director of the Bennington Writing Seminars and editor of the journal *AGNI*, based at Boston University.

BEVERLEY BIE BRAHIC's translation of Apollinaire, *The Little Auto* (2012), was published by CB editions. Her forthcoming poetry collection is *White Sheets* (CB editions and Fitzhenry & Whiteside, 2012).

TARA BRAY's* most recent book is *Mistaken For Song* (Persea Books, 2009). She is at work on her next manuscript, "Householder."

GWENDOLYN BROOKS (1917–2000) first appeared in *Poetry* with the poems reprinted in this issue. "We Real Cool" also debuted in *Poetry* (September 1959) — "We//Lurk late. We/Strike straight."

MICHAEL COLLIER's sixth book, *An Individual History*, will be published by W.W. Norton, July 2012. He teaches at the University of Maryland and is director of the Bread Loaf Writers' Conference.

EDUARDO C. CORRAL's first book, *Slow Lightning* (2012), was selected by Carl Phillips as the 2011 winner of the Yale Series of Younger Poets competition.

PAUL DURICA is a graduate student at the University of Chicago and the founder of Pocket Guide to Hell Tours and Reenactments.

WILLIAM EMPSON (1906–1984) first appeared in *Poetry*, November 1936: "We now turn blank eyes for a pattern there/Where first the race of armaments was made."

MILTON GLASER co-founded the revolutionary Push Pin Studios in 1954 and *New York* magazine in 1968. In 2009, he was the first graphic designer to receive a National Medal of the Arts award.

GEOFFREY GRIGSON's (1905–1985) "Letter from England" was his first appearance in *Poetry* (November 1936).

JASON GURIEL is the author of a collection of poems, *Pure Product* (Véhicule Press, 2009). His writing has recently appeared in *Parnassus*, the *New Criterion*, *PN Review*, *Maisonneuve*, and *Reader's Digest*.

GEOFFREY HILL's first poem in *Poetry* (May 1957) was "Wreaths," reprinted in this issue.

SEAN HILL* is the author of *Blood Ties & Brown Liquor* (UGA Press, 2008). His awards include fellowships from Cave Canem and the MacDowell Colony. He lives in Bemidji, Minnesota.

CLIVE JAMES's latest books are *Opal Sunset* (W.W. Norton, 2008), *The Revolt of the Pendulum* (Picador, 2010), and *The Blaze of Obscurity* (Picador, 2009).

PATRICIA KIRKPATRICK* has published *Century's Road* (Holy Cow! Press, 2004) and books for young readers, including *Plowie: A Story from the Prairie* (Harcourt, 2004).

NATE KLUG's first chapbook, *Consent*, was published by Pressed Wafer this spring.

YUSEF KOMUNYAKAA's most recent collection of poetry is *The Chameleon Couch* (Farrar, Straus & Giroux, 2011). He teaches at New York University.

MAXINE KUMIN, former US poet laureate and winner of the Pulitzer and Ruth Lilly prizes, is the author of seventeen volumes of poetry. She lives on a farm in New Hampshire.

KAREN AN-HWEI LEE is the author of *Phyla of Joy* (Tupelo Press, 2012), *Ardor* (Tupelo Press, 2008), and *In Medias Res* (Sarabande Books, 2004). She lives and teaches in southern California.

DAVID LEHMAN's most recent collections are *Yeshiva Boys* (2009) and *When a Woman Loves a Man* (2005), both published by Scribner.

HAILEY LEITHAUSER has recent or upcoming work in *AGNI Online*, *Antioch Review*, *Gettysburg Review*, *Subtropics*, and *Triquarterly Online*. She lives in Silver Spring, Maryland.

PATRICIA LOCKWOOD's first book, *Balloon Pop Outlaw Black*, is forthcoming from Octopus Books in July.

WILLIAM LOGAN's most recent book of poetry, *Strange Flesh* (Penguin), was published in 2008. His edition of the forgotten poem *Guy Vernon*, by John Townsend Trowbridge, will be published this spring.

ANTHONY MADRID lives in Chicago. His first book, *I Am Your Slave Now Do What I Say*, will be published by Canarium Books this spring.

AMIT MAJMUDAR's poetry collections are *o',o'* (TriQuarterly Books, 2009) and *Heaven and Earth* (Story Line Press, 2011).

HOWARD NEMEROV (1920–1991) first appeared in *Poetry* in August, 1943. He had nearly one hundred poems published in the magazine.

KATHY NILSSON* lives in Cambridge, Massachusetts, with her husband and son. Her first book, *The Infant Scholar*, is forthcoming from Tupelo Press.

VERA PAVLOVA was born in Moscow. She is the author of seventeen collections of poetry and five opera librettos. Her first collection in English is *If There Is Something to Desire* (Alfred A. Knopf, 2010).

V. PENELOPE PELIZZON's first book is *Nostos* (Ohio University Press, 2000). She is also co-author of *Tabloid, Inc: Crimes, Newspapers, Narratives* (Ohio State University Press, 2010).

MURIEL RUKEYSER (1913–1980) first appeared in *Poetry* in April 1933: "O strong unlove against our fellows here,/Never again set me so high, away/From action."

STEVEN SEYMOUR is a professional interpreter/translator who has worked for years as a contractor to the US State Department at the Geneva negotiations on nuclear arms control and disarmament.

SANDRA SIMONDS is the author of *Warsaw Bikini* (Bloof Books, 2009) and *Mother Was a Tragic Girl* (Cleveland State University Press, 2012).

PATRICIA SMITH is the author of eight books, including *Blood Dazzler* (2008) and *Shoulda Been Jimi Savannah* (2012), both published by Coffee House Press.

GERALD STERN's most recent books are *Stealing History* (Trinity University Press, 2012), "a sort of record of a mind in the year 2010," and *In Beauty Bright: Poems* (W.W. Norton, 2012).

WENDY VIDELOCK lives in Western Colorado. Her book, *Nevertheless* (2011), is available from Able Muse Press.

* First appearance in *Poetry*.

In the Library

CHILDREN'S EVENTS

Toddler Poemtime

Wednesdays, 11 am

Children ages 3 to 5 are invited to a weekly storytime event that introduces poetry through fun, interactive readings and games. Admission is granted on a first come, first served basis.

Elementary Poemtime

January 11, February 8, March 14, April 11, 4 pm – 5 pm

Students in grades 2 to 4 are invited to a monthly hour of poetry reading featuring age-accessible poetry, crafts, and games. Admission is granted on a first come, first served basis.

Teen Book Club

January 4, February 1, March 7, April 2, 4 pm – 5 pm

Students of all experience levels currently enrolled in grades 9 to 12 are invited to a monthly poetry discussion group. In a conversation moderated by Poetry Foundation youth services assistant David Gilmer, teens discuss well-known classics as well as contemporary work. The Teen Book Club strives to develop and refine each participant's ability to read, understand, and appreciate poetry. All participants will engage with the month's reading and assess its impact on their lives. Space is limited to 15 participants. Please register in advance by e-mailing: library@poetryfoundation.org.

LIBRARY HOURS:
Tuesdays, Thursdays & Fridays, 11 am – 4 pm

Children Only Hours:
Wednesdays: 10 am – 5 pm; Toddler Poemtime 11 am

61 WEST SUPERIOR, CHICAGO
(312) 787-7070 • poetryfoundation.org

POETRY OFF THE SHELF

Poesía en Abril

Susurros, or whispers, is the theme of the fifth edition of the Poesía en Abril festival, a celebration of Spanish-language poetry. Miguel Barnet of Cuba and Ana Rossetti of Spain appear for a bilingual reading and performance. Co-sponsored by *contratiempo*, Instituto Cervantes, and DePaul University.

SATURDAY, APRIL 7, 7:00 PM
POETRY FOUNDATION | 61 WEST SUPERIOR STREET

Dark Room Collective

The celebrated Dark Room Collective reunites for a special reading featuring Thomas Sayers Ellis, Nehassaiu deGannes, Major Jackson, John Keene, Sharan Strange, Natasha Trethewey, and Kevin Young.

THURSDAY, APRIL 12, 7:00 PM
POETRY FOUNDATION | 61 WEST SUPERIOR STREET

Poetry & Piano

Poets Averill Curdy, Calvin Forbes, Coya Paz, and Roger Reeves and pianists Adam Marks and George McRae collaborate for an evening of music and poetry. Co-sponsored with PianoForte Foundation, Borderbend Arts Collective, and Experimental Piano Series.

SATURDAY, APRIL 14, 7:00 PM
CURTISS HALL | FINE ARTS BUILDING
410 SOUTH MICHIGAN AVENUE

POETRYFOUNDATION.ORG/EVENTS

BACK PAGE

April 1950

In August 1949, Foote, Cone & Belding, on behalf of its client, Marshall Field & Company, purchased twelve full-page, inside-cover advertisements in *Poetry* at ninety dollars apiece. The contract brought together three Chicago institutions. Housed in the Palmolive Building (later home to *Playboy*), Foote, Cone & Belding held the accounts for such prominent brands as Kleenex and Levi's. Marshall Field's had been the city's premier department store since the Great Fire of 1871. For *Poetry*, the sales promotion office of Marshall Field's produced an especially tailored series of advertisements. Beginning in November 1949, readers encountered products proclaimed to inspire sonnets, epics, madrigals, and so forth. "Inspiration for a Ballad" is the second-to-last of these advertisements to appear in print. Foote, Cone & Belding abruptly terminated the contract, with five ads remaining, that month. By April 1950, *Poetry* was already engaged in the postwar sale of literature as an experience. The issue also contains a quarter-page ad for Kenyon College's School of English, a precursor to contemporary summer seminars and workshops. Among the lecturers whom paying students were promised to encounter at Kenyon is Delmore Schwartz, the issue's featured poet.

Paul Durica

"Back Page" is a monthly feature of artifacts from the last one hundred years of *Poetry*.

inspiration for a ballad

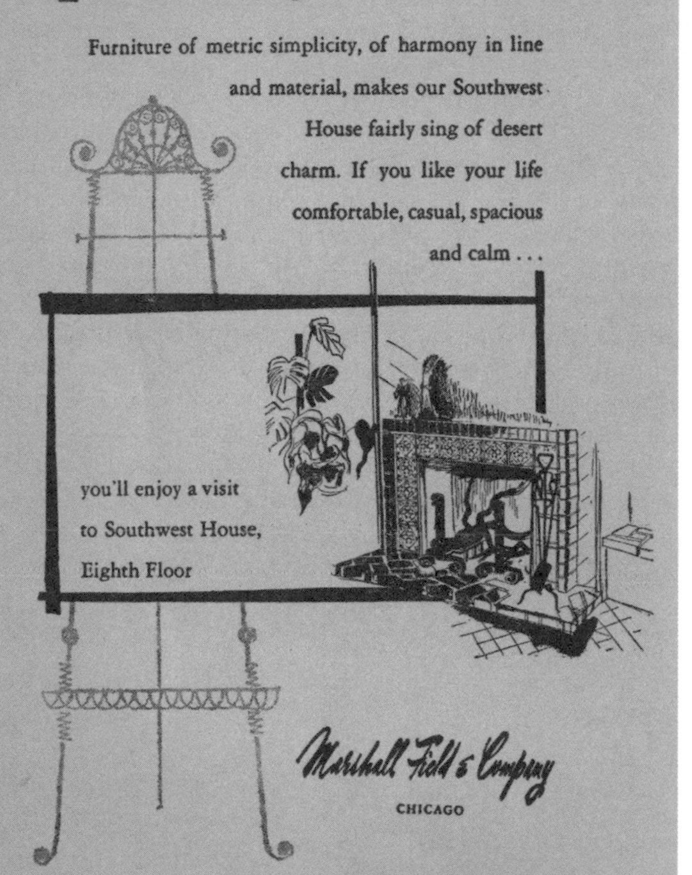